SNOW IN APRIL

Snow in April

CARL J. NELSON

WIPF & STOCK · Eugene, Oregon

Wipf and Stock Publishers
199 W 8th Ave, Suite 3
Eugene, OR 97401

Snow in April
By Nelson, Carl J.
Copyright©1966 by Nelson, Carl J.
ISBN 13: 978-1-60608-913-2
Publication date 8/01/2010
Previously published by Hunter Press, 1966

A collection of meditations

CONTENTS

A Longing	15
Within Myself	17
Like Astronauts In Space	18
Man Alive	20
Who?	22
Sunshine	25
The All Important Link	26
Glint Of Firefly	28
A Lengthy Conversation	30
Anonymity	32
Summer	33
Crimson Stain	34
The Dark Of Nights	36
Quietly To Persist	38
Trust	40
Erect And Confident	43
To Be Myself	44
Fitful Wisps Of Smoke	46
No Trail Is On The Sea	48
A Sweeter Wine Of Life	50
Caught Red-Handed	52
An Olden Time Town Crier	54
Release To Be Myself	56
The Glory And The Flame	58
Why Is It?	59
Myself Externalized	60
My Erstwhile Enemy	62
Work Of Art	64
Men Are Story Tellers	66
February	68
Self-Possessed	70
In The Hearts Of The People	72
Sustain This Star	75
My Valedictory Oration	76
We Emoted	78

A Middle Way	80
The Holy Land	82
Point Of View	84
A Subterfuge	86
A Mote Of Dust	88
Multitudes Of Men	91
The Structuring Of Power	92
Never Try Dividing	94
The Universe Going Visiting	96
The "I" In Me	98
The Strength To Dare	100
In Memoriam	102
My Internal Hearth	104
Narcissus-Like	106
Fiercely Jealous	108
Birds Are Singing	110
Cooling Fingers Through My Hair	112
I Must Stand Alone	114
A Cricket Singing Selflessly	116
In That Searing Agony	118
The Full Estate Of Man	120
I Judge Myself	122
Snow In April	124
To Brim With Life	125
The Seas Within	126
Phoenix-Like	128
When Desert Wastes Begin To Bloom	130
Silent Centuries Speak	132
To Pass The Test	134
A Mood Of Merriment	136
A Work Of Art	138
Laugh Or Cry	140
Joyously Possessed	143
Wings Of The Spirit	144
So Swing	145

SNOW IN APRIL

A LONGING

A longing
broods through space and endlessness of time.

Out of the flame of bursting stars,
out of the swirl of cosmic dust,
out of deluging waters,
life emerged upon the earth.
At its behest,
living things rejoice for their brief moments.

Here I stand a creature,
yet still in process of creation.
I am,
and yet I am becoming.
There is no end,
for when all is said and done,
when the shouting and the tumult in my life subsides,
still -- still there will be a longing.

I yearn for an identity --
to spell the letters of my name --
to mark upon the universe
the length and breadth of my domain --
to stretch up high the roof above my dwelling place
and sink foundations deep into the rock of understanding.

But poignancy forever taints my joy;
a vague unrest disturbs my satisfaction in achievement;
mystery lays its fingers on my lips,
hushing words of braggadocio.

An insistent urge attempts to bring to birth
a beauty in my soul,
to gather threads of interest
and weave them into purpose.

    Yet who am I and why --
how can I answer?
    Chaos
forever curtains my beginnings,
and the void of the unborn
forever blankets out the future.

    Whoever I might be,
yet I know I am the creature of an overwhelming ardor,
    Wherever I might be,
yet I am filled with yearning.

    Man is a lonely creature of the stars;
eternity blows cool upon his cheek;
and though he should blast his dwelling place
into a cloud of dust,
yet there will be
a longing.

WITHIN MYSELF

The meadow gleans its greenness
from each shooting blade of grass.
The forest musters up its windy roar
from voices of each singing tree.
Humanity collects its purpose
from ideals of each aspiring man.
Thus larger characters are but collections
of the industry of many selves.

If society has faults,
I only see my own shortcomings multiplied.
If my world is to improve,
it is I who must improve;
for I am not responsible for other lives,
only my own.

The most terrible of crimes
are those committed by my hands.
The most evil thoughts
are those that flash upon my mind.
The most consuming hatreds
are those that burn within my heart.
For the greatest evils in the world
are those most near to me --
those within myself.

But also in my heart
may light the warmest flame of kindliness;
in my thought may flash profoundest wisdom;
by my hands
some pilgrim may be helped along the walk of life.

Here, within myself,
I must start the shaping of the world to come.

LIKE ASTRONAUTS IN SPACE

An eternal restlessness
disturbs mankind.
Not satisfied by merely gratifying needs,
man seeks for something more.
Not knowing what he seeks,
still disquietude afflicts his idle moments.

Not only must he probe
the murky darkness of the sea's abyss,
but he must challenge ramparts
arching far in outer space.
Not only must he peer
into the private lives of atoms,
but he must tune his ear to noise of galaxies
far beyond the vision of his telescopes.
The music of his voice is not enough,
but man extends the ranges of his vocal cords
in symphonies of instruments.

He digs into the earth for relics of his past,
and pries the rocks apart for evidence of ancient life.

Man converts resources of the earth
to fill his needs,
amalgamates the elements in combinations new to nature,
and refines extensions of his mind and body.

A malaise forever drives man to idealize,
devising schemes of things as yet unborn.

But despite his restless search for knowledge,
despite his aim to dominate the world,
despite his ceaseless striving to control his destiny,
despite attempts to rise above his nature,
yet earth and air will reabsorb man's body;
realities will crush his dreams to dust;
inconsistencies confound his knowledge;
enigmatic mysteries, opaque and brooding,
veil the past and future from analysis.

Though it seems that I must seek,
yet all returns
into the cornucopia of life.

Even though some place
there may be a golden apple,
yet to where could I abscond with it?

So if I must,
let me strive,
but not with vanity,
for all accomplishments of life of ages past
support my present being,
like the earth supports a launching pad;
and all the vim of life from immemorial time
empowers me,
like astronauts in space.

MAN ALIVE

In Memory of Albert Schweitzer

    As man alive
I rejoice in all my body --
in its progressive gains and limitations.
    As man alive
I accept tragedy, disease, and misery
as challenge to my perseverance.
    To all that touches my awareness
I shout a thundering "yes"
that shakes foundations of the earth
and startles even stars,
so that their twinkle ceases,
and they clutch the heavens
lest they be shaken to the earth
like decorations from a Christmas tree.

    With all my being --
by example, word, and deed --
I say "Yes."
    Down all the empty avenues of space,
resounds my "Yes."
    Through echoing halls of time
reverberates my "Yes."
    To war, calamity, and pestilence,
to death, defeat, frustration, disappointment --
to all that I consider evil,
I say "Yes."

Yes, and more.
Beyond this I say "Yes"
to the ennoblement of man --
"Yes" to an awakening empathy --
a concern to help, to aid, assist.
"Yes" to human sentiment
that leads the way to brotherhood.
"Yes" to love where hate prevailed before.
"Yes" to concern
where indifference may have ruled.
"Yes" to humanizing
all the world of man.
And "Yes" to a reverence
for all the world of living things.

Time will weather my foundations soon enough;
neglect will atrophy, accident destroy,
competition will suppress.
I need not set in motion forces that destroy,
for they are numerous and strong enough.
But only I can build my character;
and only men can build humanity.

I am what all the ages have affirmed --
no more, no less.
Beyond this wealth of my inheritance
what is distinctly me will be what I affirm --
no more, no less.
And living in the future will become
the total of what we each affirm --
no more, no less.

WHO?

Who is my mother,
father, brother, sister?
And who,
in truth, is not?

Is not a mother, father, brother, sister
only I in some other guise?

Who can fathom
the mysterious process
giving life to each -- a sense of singularity?
Somewhere
in the misty meadows of antiquity
human races slowly drew apart,
assuming an identity,
even as I now assume identity among my fellows.
And today I see the many races of the world!
Africans,
who struggle for a national identity;
Chinese
who labor to ward off
the grinning skeleton of famine;
Russians
laboring to humanize a tyranny;
East Indians
striving for material necessities
to supplement the spiritual;
Americans
seeking spiritual necessities
to supplement materials --
all people
are reflections of myself.
"There", I murmur,
"but for vicissitudes of fate,
am I."

Somewhere
still further back into the stream of life,
man separated from the other creatures of the earth.
  Contemplating all these hosts inhabiting the earth --
the swimming, creeping, flying;
the large and small;
the swift and slow --
contemplating all of these
again I say,
"But for vicissitudes of fate,
there am I."

  Still relatedness continues,
for somewhere in the wholeness of it all
moving creatures separated from the green;
once animals and plants were one.
  My head must bow before this truth,
and I must say,
"This blade of grass,
but for vicissitudes of fate,
is I."

  Yet mystery deepens still.
  Who can draw the line
between these cells of mine
and atoms of the air?
  Physicists demur,
for at a point his lifeless atoms
seem to come alive;
and biologists must hesitate
for at a point his living cells
seem to be inanimate.
  Yes, I am even kin
to atoms of the earth and air.

    Who can draw the line?
    Who is my mother, father, brother, sister,
for I am relative to all that has, and does and will exist.
    I can only ask,
"Of all my relatives,
of all the hosts of this creation past and present,
who is my nearest mother, father, brother, sister?"

SUNSHINE

I am;
I am processing
for good or evil.
   The world is not hostile,
nor does it lead one by the hand;
it simply offers endless opportunity
for self-achievement or for self-destruction.

   Faith, then,
seems the part of wisdom.
   The young, mature, the old --
all men yearn for someone's trust;
and that trusting is a shining sun in which they grow.
   Like plants
that turn their leaves
toward the warming rays of sun,
all men look to that which gives them confidence.
   Trust is a light
that smiles encouragement.

   Faith
can soften hatred into love,
broaden ignorance into wisdom,
gainfully employ a former criminal.

   Faith has many facets;
as hope, it is the arm of help;
as trust, it is the base of triumph;
as confidence, it is the steel of competence.

   Faith is sunshine;
nothing grows without it.

THE ALL IMPORTANT LINK

A presence
inflames the universe.
A pervading power
continually refines the features of mankind.
A livingness
enlivens atoms, earth, and galaxies;
and most important to myself,
enlivens me.

But the magic working of creation
shimmers only in existent things.
Each part and particle of the universe
merits wonder and amazement.

A stone upon my hand
contains a treasury of secrets.
Raindrops splashing on my cheek
will ever bring surprise.
Trees swaying in the wind
express the mystery of life.

Rise my soul,
accept the challenge!
Tense every fibre of this body
to meet the unexpected!
Alert the sense
that each moment may be relished!
Endure the suffering
that may come my way!
And eventually challenge death
to obliterate the uniqueness of my having been,
if it can!

Meaning comes to those
who rise up to the challenge,
who weather gracefully with time,
who take the consequence of change
by yielding to experience,
and in their wake
leave evidence of having been.

For in the past
is stored the monuments of those
who, throwing caution to the wind,
confronted the unknown.

The future is the formless stuff
of which I fashion meaning;
I cannot find it there
already made.

I stand between the future and the past,
and looking back
upon the life that I have lived,
upon the history of the race,
and the whole of life,
meaning gleams in countless multitudes
of lives, events, accomplishments.

Yes, I stand between the future and the past,
the all important link between the two,
and having been,
I can never be
undone.

GLINT OF FIREFLY

Institutions
preserve a status quo
often sancitifed as holy
by those who serve them
and to whom they give a vested interest.

Once established
their servants sometimes seek
to stifle freedom,
belittle critics,
ignore just grievances,
decry the uninitiated.

But
what men create
must yield and change
as they reflect the changing needs of living men.

Their individuality
is the hope of men;
this mote of dust,
this echo in the wind,
this single glint of firefly in darkness of eternity,
this self-propelled, self-willed,
lonely loneness
is the salvation of the world.

Yes,
I must muster courage
of my aloneness.
  It is an awesome task
to pit my inconsequence
against the mighty walls of state.
  It may seem impertinence
to challenge the decisions of the rulers.

Knees may tremble
when, unarmed, one may face a brutal, armed police.

   But people are the state;
people are the great resource
of truth, invention, rectitude;
people generate, renew, revise, enlarge;
people are -- they need no reason to exist.

   If institutions
over-ride initiative of men,
they become but outward shells,
a crushing burden,
restricting freedom,
encouraging retreat, apprehension, fear,
defeat.

   But as people
take upon themselves direction of an institution,
it becomes a strengthening skeleton
for their freedom, dance, and song.

   My individuality
is the salt of earth --
the light
upon the hill.

   By exerting that,
I make my institutions
a skeleton within my freedom,
rather than the shell
of my imprisonment.

A LENGTHY CONVERSATION

Must I
be forever noisy, garrulous,
thinking I communicate by words alone?

Perhaps the problems of the world
would faster reach solution
if men,
but for a day,
ceased their shouting,
relaxed their vocal cords,
closed their lips
and listened!

In a calm enveloping the world,
in a quietness with all humanity
attentively attuned to hear
though no one spoke --
in such a silence,
men would sense a deeper form of speech --
a feeling of inclusion,
a sense of unity,
a cosmic consciousness.

Too often words, like bricks
are thrown at one another --
something which we duck,
fend off,
or craftily evade.

But the calm acceptance of another
without my presence thrust upon him
and without my calling his attention to himself
is the speech of silence.

To silently acknowledge others
without conditions,
without questions,
without comment
crys aloud of human fellowship,
and of a unity infusing all the living universe.

It is a speech so personal between us
that I seemingly ignore your presence --
pretend that you do not exist --
observe an object in the opposite direction far away.

Yet,
by quietly remaining near,
seemingly oblivious,
there is communication --
relatedness made evident and obvious.

And then,
without a word,
without notice,
without a token of good-bye,
I can leave
knowing that we have shared
a lengthy conversation.

ANONYMITY

Flushed with fervor of my high ideals,
I would fashion all the world according to my thinking;
energized by electrifying flashes of my insight,
I would declare to all creation these eternal truths.

But when these brilliant stars may fade away,
I find they are not guiding beacons
but blinding lights.
For my universe encircles
only that which I can feel and see and hear.
My experience encompasses
but a tiny portion of the total,
whatever ALL the universe may be.

But my kingdom lies within the ken of my experience
and whatever influence I have beyond those limits
works its way unknown to me.
Though I may have a larger self,
yet to me it is anonymous.

He who seeks his greatness in himself
will be great in his anonymity.
But he who seeks his greatness
in the eyes of all the world,
will be pauper
both within himself and to the world.

I do not own the world,
I possess only what I take into my being
in appreciation.

Though I have truths to share,
they are not for me to publicize;
and though I solve a world-wide problem,
yet I will never know the resolution.

SUMMER

Summer is a season of fluidity.

After being wrapped against the cold in winter,
summer is the flinging of one's coat aside,
the opening of doors and windows
and of arms to wind and sun.

Where once bare limbs were etched against the sky,
now foliage of trees uplifting sweep and weave.
Where once the tawny stalks of last year's grass
lay prostrate,
now breezes billow over waving fields of standing hay.
And in the mountains
where ice immobilized the lakes,
now waves dance and shimmer in the sun.

This is a time of flowing --
when the air is freighted with a fragrance,
when clothing flaps and swoops on clothes lines,
when sail boats flutter over lakes and rivers,
and swallows skim the water
and, veering, soar into the air.

One can almost see
rose buds open petals to the sun,
corn stalks rise in rapid growth,
and fledgling robins clothe themselves
and spread their wings.

Colors melt and flow
from red to pink, to blue and yellow
in countless banks of flower beds.

For it is a time of flowing,
of delight in new found freedoms
of the body, mind, and spirit.

CRIMSON STAIN

    Struggle by my forbears
bought my liberties.
    Death and suffering
of men lost in the past
bequeathed to me my liberty.

    I vacillate
in my convictions.
    War is evil;
bloody conflict I abhor;
and yet my liberties of speech and worship,
the freedoms I enjoy from want and fear,
were bought by lives extinguished violently.
    The acrid smell of gunsmoke of two centuries ago
permeates my right to vote.
    The red stripes of my flag
are pale reminders of the blood
spilled that people's representatives and courts
might rule this land.

    But in the end
have I a choice
of freedom without struggle?

    Humanity is part of life
and life is often brutal.
    What is humane
must be maintained
against a universe indifferent.
    Life must struggle with environment;
man contends with elements
and other forms of life;
men often wrestle with each other,
and I must fight with all of these
and also with myself.

    I can only hope
that violence will be contained;
that war may never be repeated;
that injury may never be deliberate.

    Still struggle is the price of freedom;
and only I
in the privacy of my person
can set its price;
but if blood-shed seals the bargain,
in respect for liberty of others,
its crimson stain
must ooze
from me.

THE DARK OF NIGHTS

When I have quieted my striving
and stilled
the clamor of my senses,
eventually,
in time,
I feel a presence
without form.
It flows
from far beyond the years and centuries.
It splashes over
cubicles of space.
It is a namelessness
that flows within me, through me, and around me.
In it I live
and move and have my being.

It is like
the sea beneath the waves,
the atmosphere around the storm,
the light of days,
the dark of nights.

It seems
as soft as water,
as indistinct as whispers,
as formless as the air.

It is shy as snowflakes melting on one's hand,
retiring as stars in daylight,
persistent as is silence.

It is like
the joy behind my smiles,
the bitterness behind my tears,
the hope behind ideals.

It has no outwardness,
only inwardness.
It cannot be seen,
or heard,
or touched.

But still it fills my being.
Nothing can exist without it,
and yet nowhere
is it found.

QUIETLY TO PERSIST

Rome
was not built in a day,
it is said;
nor can I plant an acorn in the morning
and sit in the shade of an oak
that afternoon.

And yet I often feel
my efforts ought to shake the earth;
but imagine
all the shattering convolutions of our planet
if each shaker of the earth should have his way.

No,
I am one among the millions in the present
and billions of the past.
  Each is destined to significance
but somewhat in proportion to one's fraction of the total.

Because this day is mine,
the past may seem more bright --
the future more alluring.
  Because I am familiar with this place,
other pastures may seem greener --
other ends and aims more beckoning.

But this day,
to me so ordinary,
is all the past has had to work with
and all the future can expect.
  This place
made common by familiarity
is the only place that I can ever be.

And though my days may seem quite plain,
yet over years
they have accumulated something precious.
   This place
so common in experience,
has borne its fruit unnoticed.

   Quietly to persist --
not tugging, fretting, straining,
then stamping off in righteous indignation
as when the earth in turning on its axis
does not at my command speed up --
but enjoying all my days and place,
grateful for the smaller favours in my life,
forbearing any grandiose endeavours,
accepting now this time, this place --
thus will I gain my best rewards.

   For eternity goes on forever;
hurrying will never get me there or anywhere
the sooner.
   And space
is a big, big, place --
so big my arms and fingers
stretch out straight on either side
when I try to grasp
and shake it.

TRUST

There are the things I know --
the things that I can see and taste and feel.
A host of facts --
carefully dissected,
separated, catalogued, and labeled --
rest on library shelves.

But too
there are the things I do not know --
things not as yet resolved --
passive things opaquely lying on my hand --
things lost in the immensity of space and time.
But face to face with the unknown,
I must still be trusting.

Like sand,
our knowledge comes in bits and pieces,
We know
that living things are splintered
into hosts of species and genera.
Multitudes of men
proceed upon their separate ways.
Fragments of matter
scattered through immensities of space
flame in lonesome stars,
and speed within the atom.

Yet,
in spite of this diversity
unity infuses all that is.
An inward magnetism
attaches each to all.
Facts cannot tell me,
this I must believe.

I know that men
have not as yet emerged from savagery --
that greed and hate
still blotch our hands with brutal deeds.
    Yet I believe
that men respond to courtesy and trust.
    History may show the opposite;
yet I believe that gentleness will win the day.

    To me
truth seems to stand upon a hill
and shout and wave its arms,
it seems so obvious.
    Yet I believe
it seems the same to others.
    I believe all sentient things
experience truth as clearly as do I.

    Thus with such a trust
among my multitude of facts,
I find a union threading them together.
    Through the vast mysteriousness beyond my ken
I find a unity.

    For what is life
but trust in strangeness?
    What is life
but an eagerness to search,
trusting that my findings will be friendly,
or if hostile,
at least not consciously malicious.
    What is life
but confidence before the unresolved?

But the spice of life is lost
if I must frisk mysteriousness
in the glaring light of knowledge
before I venture forth.

To live
one must believe.
Knowledge is not enough,
for life is lived by faith --
a trust
in the unknown.

ERECT AND CONFIDENT

I have need for wholeness --
to be one with all of life --
to be faithful to the universe.
I have need to trust,
to stand erect and confident
before the mystery of life.

When I can look on any other man on earth
and say, "There am I",
then will I have faith.

When I can thrill to the blue sweep of windy sky,
the cascading foliage of wooded hills,
the smile of waving fields of grain --
when I want to sweep it all into my arms
and crush it to my heart,
then I am trusting -- I am whole.

When I feel the ocean breakers pulsing in my veins
and draw the granite rock I stand upon
into every bone and fibre,
then I am one with nature.

When I lose myself in all that is about me,
then I have trust
for there is nothing left to distrust.

I am whole
not because I trust this human frame alone,
but because my sense of selfhood has enlarged
and the universe and I are one.

TO BE MYSELF

An umbilical cord is cut
and another person comes into the world --
separate, distinct, unique --
destined to a shade of loneliness,
and to struggle for the mastery of nostalgia
for one's previous inclusion in the source of life.

But I am one,
distinct and lone;
and since my separation
from the source of life is irrevocable,
I only hope that I am known
for what I am,
nothing more.

To be understood --
not that others must agree,
not that I must be accepted,
not that others must approve,
but simply to be understood for what I am --
this is my great concern.

To be myself;
to mold creations with these hands uniquely mine
which can never quite be duplicated
in all the time to come;
to think some thoughts,
imperfect though they be,
which only my experience can think;
to feel some warmth
for people and for living things
that can fill no other heart in this particular way;
to thrill to effervescent beauty
that can never be repeated
in quite the same appreciation in another.

Not that what is mine is something great,
nor that others may not do it better,
but this is me,
and I am my most obvious responsibility.

To be myself --
fully, openly, completely --
within my limits and abilities;
this is the best that I can do,
and for themselves,
all I ask of others.

FITFUL WISPS OF SMOKE

In Memory of Dag Hammarskjold

Delegates of the United Nations filled the Assembly
and yet a single vacant seat
yawned
until an emptiness
pervaded all the hall --
a hall in which the previous clamor for self-interest
echoed now in sharp self-consciousness,
and harangues for world dominion,
thundering deafeningly,
bounced from wall to wall.

A room filled to capacity seemed strangely hollow
by a single empty
seat.

Many causes
flourish and then fade away
when a leader leaves the scene.
   Empires
rise and fall
with the aegis of a conqueror.
   Nations
fete their heroes
and then some day must mourn their death.
   But now
a world
has centered grief upon a common loss.

The wreckage of a plane
has written the concluding chapter of colonial designs;
fitful wisps of smoke
reveal the substance of unbridled seeking for oneself;
gray listless ashes
display the impotence inherent in unregulated power.

But must the truly great among us
be forever sacrificed
upon the altar of man's senselessness?
　　Must tragedy
forever need to strike,
like lightening,
a livid wound into man's conscience
to check each generation's selfishness?

　　Ironically
the great are greater in their graves;
and years of separation from the present
seem to lend a lengthening significance to their lives.

　　Then take to heart, O world, your loss,
and in the lengthening perspective of our time
revere the cause of human understanding
for which a brave and dedicated man
risked and lost
his life.

NO TRAIL IS ON THE SEA

Awakening
to consciousness, I find
that I already am.

Suddenly --
with no request from me,
or consultation with my wishes,
no merit on my part,
no payment,
or even the suggestion of a loan with collateral --
I am the pilot
of this ship I call myself.

It almost seems
as though the piloting is what is really me,
for all the rest is free
and I have no sense of being
before my ship was launched.

Sails billowed lazily to catch a freshening breeze;
dancing waves sparkled in the distance;
white pony clouds pranced through a bright blue sky;
a gust of wind,
a roll of ship,
a drift of rudder,
and, lo, these burning hands are mine
that counter-twist the shock upon the wheel.

Where to?

Sky and sea melt into grayness
with no hint of land or port.

Where from?

Dawn breaks upon an empty sea.

A glance
to starboard and to port
complete the circle of a shoreless sea.

In panic,
an impulse spreads alarm to rush below the decks,
pull down the hatch,
and let the ship drift where it may
at the whim of calm and storm.

But if I quell
this internal riot and stay on deck,
what shall I do?
Shall I grimly sail into the sunset,
chart the stars,
and plot my progress on a map marked off in squares?
Shall I take pleasure in my system,
and rejoice in tracing out my movements,
though no trail is on the sea,
and the ocean has no shore?

Or shall I rejoice in strength
to man the wheel,
run with the milder breezes when they blow,
steer through the storm,
and in the calm,
take time to bask in sunshine, to fish, and swim,
and watch a gull wheel screaming through the sky?

But, as the days go by,
it seems more clear
that though I am the captain of this ship,
I am a pilot on a shoreless sea.

A SWEETER WINE OF LIFE

Always in the longer view of things
there is hope.
If this hour holds its cup of bitterness,
surely days to come
will press a sweeter wine of life.
If this life of mine may be short-circuited,
surely in future generations
will come to light a more compassionate humanity.
If men in senseless conflict
blast the earth into incinerated dust,
yet surely life in other galaxies
will grow to greatness,
though we failed.

From small
and barely sensate forms of life,
through challenge, change, adventure --
through flooding tropic seas, high shouldered mountains,
and bulldozing sheets of ice,
through trial, triumph, tragedy,
through arctic snow and tropic heat,
through desert, plains and jungle,
a multitude of living things
selected, changed, adapted,
strengthened, added, grew --
improved enlarged, diversified --
tested, tried, adventured --
and building on accumulated merit of the centuries
present to us, the living,
a priceless heritage.

When looking down upon this lonely self,
defined and limited within my skin,
I often feel discouraged -- without aim or purpose --
in the face of death, defeat, and tragedy.

But looking up, out and away,
the future bursts unlimited.
　　Whatever ills beset our times,
why dwell upon them since we cannot stay?
　　We move regardless of our will,
so why not yield in spirit?
　　Why pick against the pricks?

　　There is an endless time
in which to change.
　　There is unlimited potential
of what is yet to be.
　　There is a soft resilient substance
yielding to the pressures of my hands.

　　In the longer view of things,
gleams the beacon light of hope.

CAUGHT RED-HANDED

   Often
I am angered
by disloyalty, falsehood, and deceit.
   I am frustrated
by indifference of others.
   Scalding waves of hate
sweep through my being
when I see brutality or leering malice
practiced by these other people.

   "Enemies",
I shout, point my finger,
and wave my country's flag to rally some support.
   Raging at my hurt,
I would destroy all those
who may have been the cause of my displeasure.
   With their demise,
so clicks my logic,
I will be free and clean again.

   Yet though I may destroy my enemies,
though I destroy
all those in whom a trace of evil may appear,
even though I may destroy all living men upon the earth,
both good and bad,
so that no tainted person can escape
and only I remained,
yet would my enemy still live --
an enemy grown strong and brash --
a monstrous genie of iniquity
learing from my visage
and caught red-handed in _my_ crimes.

How can this be?
Let me sit down
to catch my breath,
wipe sweat from off my brow
and cool this fevered agitation.

Reflecting
on this paradox
it seems apparent
my enemies can never be destroyed,
but rather
they must be transformed to friends.
Hatred
must be pacified
and taught a trade.
Anger
must be gently led by hand
and shown the beauty of the world about us.
Frustration
must be wined and dined,
taken for an outing at the beach,
or to an evening at the movie.

I may as well declare a truce
and be reconciled that my enemies will always be.
Since they can never be destroyed
I may as well transform them into friends,
help them find employment that is peaceful,
and even fraternize a bit.

Strange,
I wonder where they may have gone?

AN OLDEN TIME TOWN CRIER

A yawning canyon gapes between myself
and these crowds of people whom I shoulder through
or dodge in order to avoid collision;
and as I think upon this paradox,
an awful loneliness
elicits some mysterious and primitive nostalgia.

Yet
this solitariness of mind
broadcasts the fact of my humanity
like an olden time town crier
shouting thunderous proclamations
over and beyond the ears of listening people;
for the whole of human kind, both past and present,
telescope into this miniature of humanity
that is I.

Further, the distinctiveness of man
proclaims the pageantry of all of life on earth
that stretches far beyond beginnings of the human species;
for without the whole of life
man could not be.

And life on earth
declares the tendency to organize
infusing all the universe;
for without a universal field of mutuality
life on earth would not be here.

Waves rolling on the ocean
take their being from the vastness of the sea.
Single blades of grass
form the green expanse of meadow.
And solitary trees
lift their branches up to form the forest's canopy.

Such things
as exploding stars, volcanoes, and the death of men
dramatize the endless, not the end;
for if volcanoes had their way the earth would not exist,
yet here it is beneath my feet.

   If exploding stars should have their way,
galaxies would not glitter in the sky,
yet there they shine.

   If death should have its way,
life would not proliferate upon the earth
yet here I am.

   It seems that a continuous creativity
infuses all of time and space --
an infinite becoming,
an eternal process of rebirth.

   And so my thoughts
approve the rectitude of earth.

   For my oneness proves my universal heritage;
and thus I find the courage in my loneliness to smile,
and in spite of death,
take heart.

RELEASE TO BE MYSELF

    Up from primeval seas
green with minute forms of life --
up from living things
struggling out of seas to conquer barren continents --
up from instincts, passions, and a fierce will to live
that structures water, air and dust into a human form,
here am I,
a man.

    And, too, about me
up from these same beginnings,
hosts of other creatures
fly and leap and swim.
    And like the fins of fish,
the eagle's wings,
the antlers of the deer,
I, too, have specialized distinction.

    I am the thinker.
    Seated,
chin upon my fist,
I muse on symbols
and give to them a meaning.
    By virtue of my mind
I am presently the ruler of the earth,
or so it seems.

    So effective is this tool of mine
that men made God a man
and gave to him the magic of the mind
with which he made creation.
    Or,
to those of other loyalties,
images already seem to be within the forms of nature
and only need deciphering.

So truth for all creation
seems to be out there, apart from me,
and yet conveniently fitting into my conceptions.

But when I interrupt my thoughts,
arise to stretch and yawn,
and walk among the host of creatures of the earth.
I wonder if to a fish the universe has fins,
or to an eagle God has wings,
or to a deer that antlers bear creation up.

Such musings make me wonder
if man's truth is relative to man alone;
but if my truth is relative to me alone,
then all others must contrive their private versions.

If this be true
then I can never truly hold dominion
over other men,
nor can mankind
maintain dominion over all creation.
And if I try
I only thwart and twist creative processes
and leave the world in which I live
that much less rich and interesting.

Though humiliating this may be,
it brings release --
release from foolish lust for power,
and release to be myself.

THE GLORY AND THE FLAME

    The glory of man is crowned with flame.
His soul is torn
by the struggle of good with evil.
    Though he is lifted to the creative heights of heaven,
yet he is dashed into the consuming fury of hell.
    Though his being reaches out
and mingles with others in love,
yet he must wrestle with hate that seethes within.

    The history of man is the history of his achievements,
but it is also the history
of his violent struggle with himself.

    In shame of man,
our mother earth has lifted cloudy hands
to hide her face.
    And in pride of man,
she has beamed and rejoiced in the sunshine.

    In hate and in war,
man has turned his sword upon himself.
    He has let his own blood;
he has mutilated his own body;
he has slashed his own limbs.
    But in love and in peace
he has bound up his own wounds;
he has exalted his talents;
he has created beauty;
he has found meaning in life.

    And I, as the son of man, am handed now
the glory and the flame of being human.
    I too must now contest
the chance of evil in myself.
    But I may also glory in the greatness
of the human enterprise.

WHY IS IT?

Living here in freedom,
I cannot understand
why people in far lands
can tolerate oppression.
Rise up, I say,
and smash your chains!

As one educated,
I scoff at those
who revel in their ignorance.
How can some people
be so stupid?

With the vigor of a well-fed body,
I am scandalized that some foreign people
seem to compromise their principles
for the bribe of food.
Surely personal integrity
cannot be bought, I say.

Secure within complete acceptance,
I am appalled
that people still can swallow
some outlandish superstition
and find it appetizing.

As one of a white majority,
it seems to me
that minorities are often over-sensitive
in regard to race and color.

Why is it
that I am one of few
to have integrity of thought,
that I am one of few
to rise above the circumstance in which I find myself?

MYSELF EXTERNALIZED

    I am a man,
and I must see creation
through the eyes of someone with my name.
    I see and feel and hear
with my eyes and ears and being.
    I sense events
through my experience.
    I measure natural phenomena
with the yardstick of my intellect.
    The universe is but myself
enlarged
like a giant shadow of my body
thrown upon a wall.

    When I denounce the faults of others,
I scourge my own shortcomings.
    When I criticize stupidity,
my level of intelligence is questioned.
    When I judge another wrong,
it is I who am in error.

    For somehow
I am part of all that is about me.
    I am free
as all humanity is free,
and chains that others wear
inevitably must drag upon my wrists and ankles.
    I am as rich as other men are rich;
I am as poor as they are poor.
    I am now exalted
as they are now exalted,
and I am now debased
as they are now debased.

    As evil is myself externalized,
so too is good.
    If beauty is to thrill my soul,
it must reside outside of me,
perchance within the colors of a sunset;
it must glow upon another's countenance;
spring from another's art in music.
    Appreciating it outside myself,
there will be beauty in my soul.

    If my ways are righteous,
I must defend the rights of other men.
    As others stand erect in human dignity,
I will stand erect.

    In my selfish interest,
let me crown the earth with glory.
    Let me accept all people of the earth,
as the image of the best within myself.
    Let me shout the joy of living;
sing praises for nobility in man;
be grateful for abundance that is mine.
    Yes,
I can create the world in which I live,
but only if I share the world I have.

    I am,
not what I think I am,
but what I think of others.

MY ERSTWHILE ENEMY

My greatest friend is not a person,
but an attitude of love in me encompassing humanity.
And my greatest enemy is not a person,
but the attitude of hate dividing people into camps
that think the other less than human.

Both lie latent deep within.
But to which shall I be host?
To which shall I appeal?

Sometimes I am the victim of emotions.
If someone glares at me
and bristles with hostility,
hate may boil my passions,
scald my better feelings, blanche my face,
and cause my hands to tremble.

But again if someone smiles
and beams in spite of my antagonisms,
I begin to mellow and feel a certain comradeship.
For who is not inclined to shed his coat
beneath the warming sunshine of good-will?

Though hate may seethe
and love may heal within my person,
I am one and still the same.
And though mankind may be divided into camps,
yet people have but one humanity
which they must share together.

Dividing lines are secondary
to the unity of all.
Our humanness takes precedence
above all other things that we might be.

This fact may loom so large
that I am unaware that it is so.
   It is like saying that the rain
that falls on other lands
is less wet than that which falls on mine;
that the skies of other countries are less blue;
that sunshine is less bright.

   But however strange another man may be,
we share a common heritage.

   There are no enemies
who cannot too be friends;
there is no evil
that cannot be redeemed;
there is no wrong
that cannot soon be rectified,
for men respond to friendliness
even as they too respond to hate.

   I have but a single enemy --
a hateful disposition.
   I have but a single friend --
an attitude of good-will.

   Thus to eliminate my seeming enemies,
I need but cultivate my better feelings,
encourage warmth to glow within my heart --
practice kindness, courtesy, consideration --
until my erstwhile enemy,
reciprocating what I feel,
becomes my friend.

WORK OF ART

Great though they be
yet the work of Michelangelo,
of Beethoven, Rodin --
pale in insignificance
before the work of art on which I labor
in my living person.

My person is a trust
lent me by the race --
a living reproduction --
an uncompleted portrait of mankind
to which I add
the colors of my passions,
the outlines of my being,
my shades of character,
my diligence and my failures.

I am an artist,
sculpturing strength into these sinews,
endurance in this constitution,
skills into these hands and feet,
alertness in these eyes and ears.

I am a tapissier who weaves
resolve into these motives,
wisdom into this consciousness,
sensitivity in these feelings,
compassion in this heart.

I am a painter
shading tones of meaning
on the human mind.

I am a musical composer
harmonizing differences
in compromise and in co-operation.

I am a poet
composing sonnets
in the attitudes of living flesh.

And finally my uncompleted work,
slightly tarnished or enhanced
will be returned into the custody
of future generations.

MEN ARE STORY TELLERS

Man
is a story teller
for he fashions splendidly unlikely legends,
transcribes his fantasies in poetry,
lives vicariously in drama,
and manipulates imaginary characters in fiction.

Somewhat unobserved
the human past has carefully hidden information
in these stories men will tell.
For by tucking truths into these narratives
the past has sent its message on to us.

Truths
are tucked in fairy tales,
masked by our myths,
woven in the fabric of our fables,
and nestled in our novels.

It is with delight
that I retell these tales,
and vaguely feel the truth that may come with them.

But I sometimes take the story
for the truth,
and do not see beyond the language
to the meaning.

I need remind myself that
a myth is but an envelope
that carries truths upon a page within;
a legend is a plane
that carries passengers from out the past;
a story is a ship --
its hold filled with the golden ore of meaning.

I need remind myself
that men are story tellers,
and the tale is but the wrappings
on the gift within.

FEBRUARY

Of all the months,
it seems that February is the most capricious,
and anyone who ventures to predict,
in February,
risks his reputation.

In this capricious month,
unguarded reference to snow
will bring an airborn avalanche.
   Or if the mercury ventures upward one degree or two,
soon it is breaking all the records
with a sirocco sweltering the land.
   Or let the mercury
inch downward but a bit
and February acting on the hint,
soon has the country in a freeze.
   Rain is as probable as snow,
in February,
and not showers either,
but a deluging flood
as though the earth were parched with thirst.
   And if the sun should cleave the clouds in two
soon it will shine so warmly
as to belie the time of year.

February has a way
of turning a suggestion into saturation,
or a hint into a hill.
   It has not learned
what moderation means.

It is not
that February is so fickle;
no,
it is just so full of fission.

It is full of volatile vitality
that needs some purposeful control.

It is something like a full-grown St. Bernard
leaping on one's lap
as though it still were just a puppy,
or like the man
who sprang upon his horse,
and in a cloud of dust,
rode off at once in four directions.

Surely it must have been of February
that Mark Twain has said,
"If you do not like the weather, just wait a minute."

Though February is not quite certain
whether it is March or January,
it is still quite ready to be either one.

It is not irresolute;
it is just so unpredictable.

It does not falter;
it just vacillates.

Though February
may fluctuate from one thing to another,
though it anticipates the starting gun
and gets half way down the track before it stops,
though it presents
ridiculously incongruous versions of itself
at different times and almost simultaneously
yet one thing may be said of February
and that is
that it is
willing.

SELF-POSSESSED

    Life
is the management of power;
and personality,
its moral guidance.

    Whether I may wish it so or not,
I emerge upon this human scene
with power thrust upon me.
    Shall I avert my eyes,
let someone else usurp my heritage,
or take it into hand?

    Whatever my decision,
there it is;
and how it is disposed must be at my direction
or delinquence.
    Inescapably
I am,
for good or ill.

    I may gain direction from a mountain,
rising massively into the sky
with snow streaked shoulders shimmering in the sunshine --
host alike to antlered elk and chipmunk,
to giant fir and lowly lupine --
oblivious to the insults of the weather,
to spiteful pummeling by rain and snow,
to enveloping by clouds,
obliteration by the night,
to taunt of stars.

    Yet,
when these distractions pass,
the morning light strikes full upon the peak,
rising sheer in still blue depths of sky,
unchanged, unmoved, unoffended,
cool, contained,
yet unavoidably apparent.

    Mightily to be --
in spite of violence and conflict
in spite of charge and countercharge,
in spite of treachery, deceit, and fraud,
of tragedy, misfortune, war --
after all the lash and froth of human passions
to stand firm upon the human scene,
self-possessed and strong against the breaking day --
a pilot butte, a compass point, a stepping stone.

    Whatever others may have done with power,
may I tightly hold the reins of mine.
    This is humanly to be.

IN THE HEARTS OF THE PEOPLE

After many intervening years
I paid respects once more to Lincoln
at his memorial in Washington.

The rows of trees
upon the outside border of two esplanades of lawn
on either side the single band of water
telescoped one's eyes upon his monument.

As I walked along
absorbing all the beauty
I noticed through the foliage
a line of buildings
butting up against the bordering trees --
gray, blocky, flat roofed monsters streaked with rust.
"U.S. Navy", said a sign;
"Ammunition Warehouse No. 8", said another.

A fence stood high beyond the trees
with three barbed wires at the top
leaning out in my direction.

Really?
Was there danger
that someone might invade those ugly buildings?
Surely there was some mistake;
and those three barbed wires leaned the other way
to keep that ugliness
out of this sanctuary holy to the nation.

But no!
They leaned in my direction.
Is nothing sacred, then, to practicality?

    Maybe not;
for any sense of sacredness,
any sentiment, any hint of loveliness
would change men's loyalties.
    It all depends which side the fence you're on;
but for me,
I'd make the wires at the top lean out the other way.
    And yet the way the wire leans
indicates the way the nation leans as well.
    Make way for progress,
though it obliterates
the things once beautiful and sacred to us.
    The pragmatic mind must ask the questions:
Does it work?
Is it useful?
Does it produce?
Make money?
    And fences must be built
to keep out disturbing questions such as:
Is it beautiful?
Is it moral?
Is it noble?
Is it just?

    I climbed the granite steps
up to the marble temple,
when a touring group of dusky, dark-eyed children
scrambled, shouting, up on either side.
    And then within,
around and underneath the kindly features
wrought in stone of Lincoln,
these dusky children laughed, played tag,
stood straight and confidently erect, or stared.

On the wall above the marble head
was this inscription:

IN THIS TEMPLE

AS IN THE HEARTS OF THE PEOPLE

FOR WHOM HE SAVED THE UNION

THE MEMORY OF ABRAHAM LINCOLN

IS ENSHRINED FOREVER

That it may be safe,
let the memory be enshrined
in the hearts of the people.
Let what is holy be enshrined
in hearts of people.

SUSTAIN THIS STAR

   A star
shining brightly
graced the night when Jesus came to birth --
so it is said.
   This child
grew up to be a man
who lived compassion, peace, good-will.
   It heralded a man
who aided those in need,
kept company with "publicans and sinners",
turned the other cheek,
forgave his executioners.

   A star
shining brightly
graced the night,
so it is said.
   It has shone
throughout the centuries
and lives of other men have added to its lustre --
Confucius, Lincoln, King,
Buddha, Gandhi, Helen Keller, Schweitzer, Hammarskjold
and countless others.
   It is the star of our humanity --
the hope of peace,
the motive of good-will.

   May this star
shining brightly
grace all nights that are to come.
   May human love
in your heart and in mine
be magnified
to sustain this star
against the night.

MY VALEDICTORY ORATION

On the long unrolling scroll of history
will this be noted as the age of words? --
when men became ideas
instead of living entities?

Will this be known
as the time when verbalization reigned as God,
and the mathematical formulae
ascended to the throne of high priest?

Will this be designated
as the age when obligations were acknowledged
with refined and proper speech,
when hollow sounding "thank you's"
became the legal tender of exchange
for voluntary human service?

In less literate times,
men of ancient lands
imbued their persons with their gratitude.
In ceremonials,
around the totem pole, to beat of tom-toms,
they danced appreciation
for the gift, and gifts, of life.
Woven into body movements --
graceful, frenzied, slow or dignified --
these men of long ago expressed their reverence.
Words were superfluous,
and only hinted at the feelings
moving in and through their beings.

    Words are my poorest form of speech;
words come so easily.
    Tumbling forth in multitudes,
they fall in line on line, sheet after sheet,
or reams and reams of paper --
words on paper stacked in books on dusty shelves --
words on paper thrown into the flames --
words on paper blowing helter skelter through the streets.
    Words are so cheap --
so easily left behind, ignored, destroyed.

    But this living flesh!
    My living self is speech
that cannot be discarded,
or filed away to gather dust,
or left to blow about the streets.
    While I am in it,
I speak with all my living presence.

    Perhaps the innocence of ages past is gone forever,
and man is too sophisticated now
to dance his thankfulness.
    But still my greatest speech,
my valedictory oration,
is spoken in this living self.

WE EMOTED

Wind forever blows to blow again.
Tides forever rise to rise again.
Spring forever comes to come once more.

The moon forever circles around the earth.
Stars speed endlessly in galaxies through space.
Electrons flee in emptiness as vast within the atom.

The world is full of sound and fury
for everything must move
and seeks an equilibrium
that can never be attained.

Persons, too, must move
from childhood through maturity to graying years.
And mankind moves
from savage sources on through history to some future race.

Yet for all the storm and violence,
for all the fiery flux and cataclysm,
for all the speed and motion,
here we are --
still here.

We move, not in a line,
but in a sense of transformation.
All the pageantry
of centuries of life on earth has been enacted,
not in some distant place,
but here beneath our feet!
We have not moved away,
but rather life on earth has been transformed
from Protozoa through the age of reptiles on to man.

We have not moved,
but rather we emoted;
not motion but emotion rules the world;
attraction changes the constituency
of all existent things.

A MIDDLE WAY

Man counts his conscience
among his many blessings;
but also he must reckon with it
as a curse of his existence.

No tribunal sits more continuously;
none demands more righteousness,
and paradoxically
none exonerates so swiftly.

Sitting in self-judgment
multiplying case on case against themselves,
men pronounce a final judgment --
one from which is no appeal.

But moral judgments are so useless,
creating the illusion that punishment absolves the crime,
or excusing one from mending harmful ways
by verdicts of "not guilty".

Let me seek a middle way
between its blessing and its curse --
not exalting in my righteousness
nor accepting all the guilt.
For a man is largely
what his circumstance have made him.
He is largely
a grand totaling of his friends and family,
his acquaintances and enemies.

So,
through the language of the heart,
of compassion and of understanding,
let me find a middle way
between the right and wrong,
the black and white,
of judgment.

Let me not convict, but correct;
not penalize, but pardon;
not blame, but build.

THE HOLY LAND

   Where is the path
that leads to the place
on which my hopes can rest?
   Where is the rock
that rises sheer
above the storming sea?
   Where is the perfect state
in which justice
rules supreme?
   Where, yes, where is the road
leading to the Holy Land?

   Anguished queries from the past
echo questions in my heart.
   Many roads have been constructed;
many promised lands have been envisioned;
many shrines have been erected,
but still the question burns,
"Where is the pinnacle
on which my hopes can light,
fold their wings,
and rest secure?"

   Yet,
in my disillusionment,
I find an answer.

   Footsore and empty handed
after traveling highways of the world,
I turn my steps toward my native land.
   And even if, upon my pilgrimage,
I find the shrine that I was seeking,
yet after homage has been made
I face about into the way I came.

And too after sauntering
through untrammeled wilderness,
at last I turn my steps to home.

Here within myself
resides the holy land.
Here within myself
can justice rule supreme.
Here within my soul
a rock soars high above the lashing sea.

And yet,
by some strange impulse
we must seek the holy land.
Perhaps it is a trek
we all should make
for shrines cannot be lived in
and after making one's obeisance
one is relieved to turn again
toward home.
The circle then becomes complete,
and all the roads that lead away
are also roads for our return.

Home
is a place of rest,
of quiet,
a sanctuary for the traveler.
It is a land made holy
by its centrality.
It is the shrine of all we are.

Search for your shrine, then,
O my soul,
that you may see upon returning
the gleaming beacon of the inner self
to which all roads outleading
also must return.

POINT OF VIEW

All men who ponder ask themselves,
"Who am I? What is really me?"

Physicists can name the atoms of the body --
carbon, iron, oxygen.
But are these really me?
No,
for I am different from a stone,
surely I am something more than dust and air.

Biologists can specify my organs, limbs, and bones.
In every part and particle
I am diagrammed and nomenclatured
like an atlas of the world.
Yet these attributes I share with many living things,
and with the hosts of my own kind.

Science cannot tell me who I am,
for men of science stand upon the outside looking in,
and I am on the inside looking out.

The point of view is all important.
The view along a roadway
seems quite different on returning
than it did upon my going.
From the inside looking outward,
only I can see things as they are to me.
It is the way in which I feel that is really me --
the width of my experience, my depth of understanding.
I am a sensing of the heat and cold,
light and darkness,
joy and sadness playing on my person.

What is really me will always be,
for inwardness
forever floods the world of being and becoming.
    Somehow I shall always have existence
in the things I love.
    Somehow I shall always be
in things that bring me joy and tears.
    I am here forever in the feelings I have known,
in the songs that I have sung,
in the triumphs I achieved,
in the failures that have brought despair.

    They have no outwardness to rust away,
no beginning and no end.
    My sensings are a wholeness
binding me to all that I experience.
    I am immortal in my feelings
as they lavish out upon this present moment
obliterating time.

A SUBTERFUGE

How is it possible
to love one's enemies?
How can I love
a brutal murderer --
someone hateful and vindictive?
How can I love
a man with human blood upon his hands
and who ghoulishly seeks out more?

Does my good-will
not stamp his actions with approval
and encourage even more aggression?

I cannot love that which to me is bad.
I will not compromise
my sense of right and wrong.
I do not like
the instruments of evil.

And so I need a subterfuge.

I will love things dear to me
so intensely
that my spirit emanates good-will
even when confronted with brutality.
Though I cannot love my enemies,
yet it is possible to love my friends and family
strong enough to over weigh a counter force.
Though I cannot compromise my principles,
yet I can exalt the positive,
seek its company,
and encourage it to grow.

It is too late
if one confronts an enemy
and has not loved before.

So drink deeply of appreciation,
O my soul,
while yet in nature's innocence.
Savour friendships
while with congenial people.
Love while you can
to build an armour of good-will
against the day of trial,
for such a day will come --
that day will come --
and I must be prepared.

Love can triumph over hate,
but only if it is familiar to one's heart
and strong by exercise.

So love the things you can
while yet you can,
O my soul,
that I might face the future confident and unafraid.

A MOTE OF DUST

    Seemingly,
from where I stand in Western life,
the universe is made of bits and pieces.
    Objects
seem to fill the universe
like grains of wheat may fill a bin.

    Objects everywhere --
like sand flung by the handfuls
into the farthest reaches of the sky;
like autumn leaves
that fall in avalanches from the trees;
like raindrops
streaking through the air to splatter on the ground;
like bits of dust
swirled up into a whirling dervish;
like flies
flitting here and there;
like numbers
racing to infinity and back;
like endless tiers of cans
stacked high on market shelves;
steps
of endless stairs;
cars
zooming by on superhighways;
planes
trailing vapor through the skies;
people, persons, walking, striding,
clicking heels on crowded sidewalks;
watches
ticking seconds, minutes, hours --
lengthened into calendars of years and centuries;
atoms, fishes, blades of grass, and stars.

Has some cosmic shotgun
blast this host of entities into being?
Has some creator
squeezed an atomizer,
spraying multitudes of parts and particles unrelated
into space?

And I --
am I an unrelated bit of flesh --
alone, forsaken, alienated --
like a mote of dust that dances
through a narrow beam of sun
and then is
gone?

Relations are subjective
and so unseen.

Unseen
the gravity that keeps the earth intact;
unseen the thread
that runs throughout my living heritage
to ancient seas;
unseen the tie
that binds me to the farthest star;
unseen the cosmic cables
holding nuclei and protons,
planets, stars, and galaxies in orbit.

Can the unseen
be less obvious
than the seen?
Parts are but pieces
of a mutuality.

    My solitariness
proves me universal.
    My person
proves humanity.
    Humanity
proves the web of life.
    Life
proves the wholeness of the universe.

    The source of things
resides within,
relating all to each
giving union to variety.

    Thus
in my loneliness,
I find comfort;
in my weakness,
strength;
in solitude,
companionship;
in anguish,
love.

    Only
as I brave the cold of loneliness
will I find the flame of meaning for my life.

MULTITUDES OF MEN

    A power,
little used,
resides within each man.
    It is seldom bold,
ostentatious or dramatic;
it has no awesome mushroom cloud above it.
    It is but a firm decision
to take a task in hand --
to put conviction to a work --
and to persist.

    If people only realized the power that they have,
instead of moaning of the senselessness of rulers,
of the avarice of vested interests,
of the darker side of human nature.
    For as we wail of all these ills,
and turn our backs upon them,
we give them lease on life.

    So peace will reign on earth
when there is peace within ourselves.
    And each need do so little,
for adding bit to bit the multitudes can have their way;
as the multitudes begin to move so will move the world.

    Pharoahs did not build the pyramids.
    No,
they were built by multitudes of men,
each doing his small share.

THE STRUCTURING OF POWER

A wind whipped mist,
a vague presence,
a formless something
looms large into my past.

Power of potential
throbs through my being --
hoary with age yet young as spring --
power without identity --
power investing all the world with glory.

Yet there is something more;
I see a complicated structuring.

I have existence
through patterns from the past.
Abandon these,
if I could,
and I would then evaporate.

Yet,
if every entity of life
transmitted only what it had received,
the wondrous structure of my body could not be,
and man and all his fellow creatures
would not now exist.

Forms are made to change --
not to worship, neither to abandon --
but to change.

A multitude of architects
industriously shape their lives.
　Each generation makes itself,
but from blueprints from the past.
　Yet this room may need enlarging, renovation,
elimination.
　A fixture may be needed here, a doorway there,
a window.
　The house may need restyling in the front,
new color schemes, a change of plantings.

　So the blueprint slowly changes through the ages,
though the buildings rise and fall.
　Styling grows more complicated
as each architect transmits his plans.

　Creation --
the structuring of power --
takes place within the present.
　For my few moments in the span of time,
I am a creator.

NEVER TRY DIVIDING

When I reflect,
I find I am a hopeless ambiguity.
I am universal
and yet unique.
I am society;
and yet I am one.
I am the all of this existence
yet gathered in the thimble of myself.

What, then, shall be my guiding light?
Shall I be selfish or magnanimous? --
that is the question.
But still further
am I magnanimous by being selfish
or selfish by being magnanimous,
that is an even greater puzzle.
For by selfishness
I develop talents and acquire property
by which to benefit mankind;
and yet sometimes my charity
may be a bribe for selfish reasons.

Reality might be a box of three dimensions;
the length I measure is the heritage of man;
the width is this society;
the depth is individual selves.

It is the point of view that differs --
the length, the breadth, the depth.

But the edges of the box recede,
the corners round,
the contours curve into a globe.
Which of the three dimensions, then,
is mankind, society, or me?

May I never be too quick
to do to others as I would have them do to me,
(they may not like my taste);
nor on the other hand may I never be too quick
to justify my selfishness on the premise
that abstinence is good (for someone else).
Somehow I must balance
helpfulness with self-reliance,
assistance with denial,
gifts with creativeness,
assurance with the truth.

Maybe I should never try dividing
what is for me,
what is for others,
and what is for posterity,
for the diameter of a globe
is the same in all directions.

Perhaps
I should simply be
in the best way possible
in all three of my dimensions.

THE UNIVERSE GOING VISITING

In my inner being glows
a fierce and ceaseless yen for freedom.

I would be free
to gain my ends,
declare my sentiments,
to be as I must be.

I would be free
from disabling want,
from constricting tyrants,
from flogging fear,
from disruption of my privacy.

I would be free,
and in the fervor of that end
I feel the world is my domain.
    My spirit ranges far and wide.
    It knows no bounds, restrictions, limits.
    All lands, all men,
all of time and space
become my private sanctuary.
    All the content of the universe
is telescoped within this single human form.

    The spirit free
is truly universal.

    And yet how curious
that though my spirit ranges far and wide,
it still resides within my skin.
    And no matter where I go,
no matter where I travel in my body,
still I cannot go beyond the confines of my skin.

I can only be the universe
going visiting,
and add a touch or two of color
to this miniature reproduction that is I.

No, I need not occupy the universe
in order to be universal.
I cannot,
even though I try.
No use subduing all the earth
in order to be free,
and to try will only bring destruction.
No use enslaving men
for then I chain myself to them
in action and reaction.

My freedom will be greatest
in freedom with my fellows.

I can only occupy my living body,
and that done well
requires all the effort I can muster.

Men confuse
the wanderings of the spirit
with the contour of their skins.
But who would want
his feet
to grow as large as the country they have traveled?

THE "I" IN ME

Obviously
I have been born.
I am a body,
physically discrete,
separate, apart, alone.

And yet through laziness,
insecurity, cowardice, or circumstance,
the "I" in me may never truly rise to take command.
My body may submit
to direction from society --
its masters, gods, conventions,
or the immediate infatuations of the crowd.
Thus I become a rubber stamp,
a broken record,
an automated product of a factory,
pre-packaged and pre-priced,
a commodity exchanged upon the market.

But for reasons I can only vaguely fathom,
the "I" in me has risen to command.
I shall be --
I shall be unique;
I shall be what only I can bring to light;
I shall direct this body
and decide
its values, purposes and products.

Yet, it is not worth the effort
if I sulk in loneliness off in my corner.
No,
and I shall not destroy the other ones I see
that I might feel more safe in my aloneness.
Nor shall I belittle the conformists,
or the people who are different.

I will not turn my back upon my fellows
and crane my neck around to cast suspicious glances
as though that I resented birth
and felt rejected
by this necessary process of creation.

   Rather, I will turn about,
wave for recognition of some persons,
and on my own initiative and power,
come to them
to share excitement and surprise
of some discovery or creation I have made

   I am no less unique,
and in that turn about,
I become a person --
one who presents himself.
   I take command,
and yet relate to humankind.
   I am self-directed,
yet a part of man.

   And in the spirit
of a new found comradeship
I will receive the gifts of others --
examine them,
set them aside in case I do not know their use
where I may ponder all the angles.
   Eventually I may discover
what they are good for,
or someone else may find them to their liking,
and in any case,
these gifts are interesting.

   In such a spirit
of exchanging presents of ourselves,
I become
a man.

THE STRENGTH TO DARE

Courage
is the inward strength of life.
Courage
is to living things
what timbered beams are to a house,
or foundation footings to a bridge.
Courage
gives an inward strength
without which life could not exist.
It lends
a stiffening stability.

Though life is transient,
yet courage
lures my deepest feelings to my consciousness.
The objects of my love may perish;
my affections may be spurned;
yet courage
dares my feelings to emerge.
Courage
risks the loss of things endeared;
for it is hardly worth the time
to live without emotion.

No work will ever be complete,
yet courage
lends a strength to sinews
straining to create.
Life's projects are unfinished
even in perspective of the ages,
let alone
in my short span of life.

Multitudes
unceasingly have labored
to enhance the human person,
so courage taunts me to improve myself
though future generations
must refine upon my handiwork.

So living is a risking,
and courage lends the strength to dare.

Yet in the larger view,
I do not risk defeat --
it is a certainty.

Tragedy looms larger
with each passing year.

Shallow optimism cannot comfort
those alive to life,
for they accept the challenge to the end.

To live constructively and graciously
with knowledge of one's ultimate demise
demands a head erect and shoulders squared.

This is the nobleness of man:
to sense the tragedy of life
and yet
undauntedly
to live!

IN MEMORIAM

John Fitzgerald Kennedy

   A nation mourns its loss --
a servant of its interests
destroyed by an assassin's bullet --
the millions robbed by one disgruntled dissident.

   A nation mourns.
   What does it mourn?
   Its people mourn a loss of self-respect.
   They mourn a light
that brightened self-esteem.
   They mourn integrity
that gave them strength to be themselves.
   They mourn an inward courage
that moved them to achievement.
   They mourn a dignity
that humanized their feelings.
   They mourn civility
that spoke respectfully to every man.
   They mourn a justice
that would not compromise on human rights.
   They mourn a parentage
that hallowed family life.

   No man is great
who does not stimulate
the inward growth of persons.
   For we share
each other's virtues
even as we share
our vice.

To love the best in others
is to build the best into ourselves,
and to build the best into ourselves
is to build it into others.

This all the great men know,
and by their inward strength
give leadership in heart
if not in mind.

Yes, within ourselves
resides the power and the glory
to shape a better world,
and though a leading light
has been extinguished,
yet may we feed the brightness
that has increased within.
May an afterglow
shine from our lives in greater strength,
ennobling humanity,
and shedding light
into our common destiny.

MY INTERNAL HEARTH

Religion is the fuel
that burns on my internal hearth
and warms my human sensitivities.

It melts the frost of conflict,
softens tension to resilience,
and reconstitutes resolve to be the man
of which the human intellect has lighted vision.

Religion's warming flame
expands the soul,
brings good cheer,
emboldens gentleness.

Religion is here to stay.

Once man felt alone
amid the seeming hostile forces of the world
and needed reassurance through religion.
Now he feels alone
amid indifferent hosts of his own kind
and needs to feel related.

It is an irony
where once man feared the unknown,
now he must be fearful of the known.
Where once he felt inadequate
to cope with nature's power,
now he feels unneeded
as gadgets and machines of his creation
bulldoze nature to submission.

Once he felt all forces were related to his person
to harm or benefit;
now he feels neglected,
disinherited, loose, and unattached.

Where once man was the victim
of easy generalities that led to hasty action,
now he is the victim
of extremely complicated diagnoses;
and after lengthy waiting for prescription
action is belated,
or he is told to go to bed
and let the experts do his thinking for him.

So religion still is man's great need --
a warmth that helps me be humane,
a warmth that gives me confidence to co-exist,
a warmth that spreads infectious cheer and optimism,
a warmth instilling courage of myself,
a warmth enlivening the whole of humankind,
the whole of life, the universe.

Religion is companion to the human mind.
At first it warmed the heart
against the threatening mysteries the mind uncovered.
Now it warms the heart
against the callousness
of a world made too familiar
by the mind's discoveries.

Religion
is an inner hearth
that warms a sense of my humanity.
It filled the needs of men of long ago;
it fills my needs today.

NARCISSUS-LIKE

As within the limits of the atom
protons and electrons swirl their separate ways,
as within the web of life
a harmony unites a multitude of living things,
as within the galaxies
a singing soars between the hosts of stars,
so a singing
resonates within the heart of me.

Let me rest my thoughts,
look gladly on this world of mine,
and sing the song that comes spontaneously to my lips --
singing only since I must,
unmindful that my song may not be heard.

Songs
are only safety valves
releasing tensions built by sadness or by joy,
like the whistling song a steaming pot may sing
as the lid blips up and down;
and the song --
the whistling steam --
can only hint at what is yet within.

But when I bustle busily about
flaunting to the world my great importance,
when I hammer nosily
to call attention to my building,
when I try to teach the world to sing my melody,
then disharmony engulfs my soul
for no one sings my song as I feel it should be sung.
While I beat the drums of my self-righteousness
and clang the cymbals of my ego,
the world seems even more awry.
I cannot lift the lid

to show the merit of my soul to others
without my powers dissipating.
   One's inwardness
can never be observed,
even through reflection to oneself.
   Power generates
within the secrecy of selves.
   Creation grows in privacy,
and I must sing as feelings generate within.

   Others cannot sing my song.
   Though I may teach them well,
yet they flat the notes,
slow or speed the tempo and slur expression.
   Others cannot sense its beauty,
and I despair
of the indifference and the callousness
of these times.

   Perhaps my song is not for me to listen to,
narcissus-like,
as sung by others.
   But as I tune my ears to hear the song of others,
a symphony reverberates through time and space --
a multitude of voices --
plumbers, clerks, accountants,
secretaries, doctors, farmers,
lawyers, nurses, janitors,
Democrats, Republicans, socialists,
pickets, businessmen, employees,
Catholics, Jews, Protestants, atheists,
black, yellow, white and red,
young and old,
children, men, and women --
hosts of voices blend into a chorus --
voices singing as they must --
each sings his song
as only each can sing it.

FIERCELY JEALOUS

Where
do the rights of man reside?

Nowhere
do I see the rights of man
emblazoned on a scroll of time.
 No generation
has yet bequeathed to progeny
the freedom they have won.
 I can find no supermarket
where rights are bought and sold.

 Human rights
seem to arise
when men stand straight and tall.
 As I demand my rights
they seem to take their shape.
 As I inscribe my name
in capital letters for all the world to see
I forge my freedom.

 Even,
as thundering waters of Niagara drive huge generators,
as gasoline explodes to power motors,
as Herculean tugs of gravity swing planets round the sun,
so too the world of man must move
by men empowered.

 Where can my rights find refuge
other than within myself?
 For all the world
is full of movement, change, destruction,
often blind and senseless,
indifferent to my aims.

But will I take command
upon this ship of state which is myself?
The storm of prejudice cannot be weathered
if I hesitate to head into the wind and waves
that would capsize my boat.

Let me, then,
in word and deed,
proclaim the rights of man.
May I be brave enough to live
the freedom I desire.
May I write down
the articles of my demands
and help to build my goals
into the institutions of the land.

Aware that what is true for me
is true for all my fellow men,
may I applaud all those who rise against great odds
to claim their rights.
May I commend
the persons who interpret laws that now exist,
for written laws are lifeless and to come alive
they must assume the flesh and bone of living men.

All things move and come alive
through power.
Only persons fiercely jealous of the rights
they share with others
can unfurl the flag
of freedom.

BIRDS ARE SINGING

From seeming time immemorial
long before my prototypes assumed the shape of man,
surely birds
were singing.

Then I appeared upon the earth;
I felt the finger of self-consciousness
point accusingly at me;
I cowered from the crack of lightning,
shrunk apprehensively from death,
placated storms with incantations,
and gained security by worshipping my gods.

But if I had listened closely,
beyond my incapacitating fear, surely
birds
were singing.

Then somewhat reassured,
I turned my fearful self-concern
into self-importance.
 So serious were my aims
that any means to gain them were condoned.
 Ancient Assyrian armies,
Persian hosts, Roman legions,
hordes of Genghis Khan,
Napoleonic legionnaires
and goose-stepping Hitlerites
have brought havoc, death, and desolation.
 But surely in the lull
between the clash of swords,
or thunder of the cannon and the burst of bombs,
the staccato of machine guns,
surely in the quiet places
birds
were singing.

    And now today
like Hercules
I seem to bear the crushing cares of all the world
upon my back.
    Human problems
beetling black like thunder clouds
threaten the foundations of the world.
    A pall of fear,
of gloom and pessimism, of terrible seriousness,
seems to blanket out the sun.

    But, if I attune my ears,
look high above my grim intent,
shed this inflated self-importance,
then I will find that still the
birds
are singing.

COOLING FINGERS THROUGH MY HAIR

For the miracle of life
I would give thanks,
but what have I to give?
   All that I am
has been inherited.
   I have but leased
the domocile of body within which I live --
a lease expiring with my death.

All the fruits of earth that fill my needs
are free but for the taking;
only men exact a charge of one another.
   And too the souls of men
are fed by beauty,
free but for the effort of appreciation.

And my creations
are reshapings of the things already here.
   I fashion metal into implements,
hew stone into my buildings,
marshal sounds to sing a melody,
and most wonderfully of all
weave water, earth and air into the temple of my body.
   But elements of earth I do not own;
they are not mine to give.

My thanksgiving must be evident
in the grace by which I live --
in my doing, hoping, thinking.

Then let the stars,
reflected,
sparkle in my eyes;
let wind
rush cooling fingers through my hair;
let earth
bestow its kiss upon my feet.

　　And let my life
reverberate a melody.
　　For the privilege of life,
let my hands be clapping,
my feet a-dancing,
my voice a-singing.
　　Let me vibrate
with the rythmic music of the spheres.

I MUST STAND ALONE

To be a person
I must stand alone --
on guard, alert and challenging --
solitary,
as though surveying all the world
upon a wild and wind-swept hill,
for many influences try to leach from me
my birth-right of integrity
to strengthen some ulterior cause.

Society
wields a whip
lashing laggards into line
and driving back the venturesome;
but one must risk the stinging lash
or lose one's individuality
in the obedience of the mass.

Power
offers promise
of achievement of my goals;
yet I must be alert
that the armored tank of power,
smashing through the opposition,
does not leave my morals
crushed
beneath its heavy treads.

Security
may lavish comfort,
and yet I may be doomed
to live within its high stone walls,
and look from my protecting fortress
through windows iron barred.

    Institutions
organize efficiently
some facets of my living,
but I must guard my conscience,
or efficiency will grease the axle of my principles
so well that no protesting squeak of friction
can be heard,
though directions change
and practices become degraded.

    Leaders
gather volunteers
to march beneath the banner of a worthy cause
yet I must keep my private purposes
or another banner may be substituted
to head the marching group.

    Yes, I must stand alone --
on guard, alert and challenging --
solitary,
as though surveying all the world
upon a wild and wind-swept hill.

A CRICKET SINGING SELFLESSLY

I am a child of earth.
My wisdom
is but a refinement of everyday truths.
My art,
the enhancement of natural graces.
Morality,
an elaboration of social instincts.

May I never forget
the elemental things,
for they are the foundation of my being.

Though aspirations soar to dizzy heights,
yet let me still enjoy
the cool and pungent smell of rain-soaked earth
on which I walk.
Though I enjoy symphonic strings,
yet may I stand entranced to listen to a cricket
singing selflessly its lonesome dirge in autumn.
Though I respond to needs of men in distant places,
let me respond as quickly
to the needs of neighbors.

Yes,
I am a child of earth.
My flesh and bone
is drawn from water, earth, and air.
My blood runs red as sunset.
My breath is but the atmosphere
flowing in and out of me.

My house is shaped from stone and wood;
my radio, directed lightning;
my government, a larger family.

And all of the world is home.

Valleys and plains are the rooms of my house;
mountains, the walls;
sunrise and sunset, the windows;
rivers and oceans, the hallways.

The light of day is my place of work;
and night, my place of rest.

Arching over all
is a roof of sky by day,
and of stars by night.

I am in and of the earth;
this is my home.

I am built
of elemental things.

IN THAT SEARING AGONY

My most devasting thought
is not that God does not exist out there,
but that ideals of mine exist,
that my purposes are real,
that creative force continues unabated every moment,
and that if God does not exist out there
then all that was attributed to him
exists in me and in mankind.

Is the glory too intense?
Is man's potential much too towering?
Are demands for nobleness so overwhelming
that I must place the glory of my being
somewhere out there
so that its light is safely dissipated?
Or is it placed out there
so I can logically deny that it exists
and thus feel more at ease
in a survival-of-the-fittest setting?

Where once it was the fashion
to believe in God,
it is the fashion now to say that God is dead,
that our universe is purposeless,
that all awaits analysis.

Ah! But I am man!
God may be dead,
but his attributes are not.
The Universe may be purposeless,
but I am not.
All things may await analysis to prove their truth,
but I do not.
I am; I live; I breathe.

Whether God out there exists
or whether he is dead
is quite irrelevant.

Neither God's existence
nor his non-existence
absolves man of responsibility.

Neither God's existence
nor his non-existence
can eclipse the glory in man's breast.

Man cannot escape morality;
Through knowledge,
man is faced with choice;

Knowing in advance what results will be,
man can fathom good and evil.

And knowing good and evil,
man is not man
unless he feels the prick of conscience.

Man is not man
unless he sometimes feels incriminating guilt.

Man is not man
unless he strives to compensate --
through service, love and understanding,
his failure to achieve his own ideals.

In spite of all my sophistry, both pro and con,
I am a moral being, knowing good and evil,
and the nobleness that can be ours
staggers the imagination.

I am doomed to guilt;
but in that searing agony
I know that I am man.

THE FULL ESTATE OF MAN

Feelings move the world;
gravity impels the flux and flow of things;
emotion is emergent motion.

But ideals are still
and lifeless without motivation;
they must be energized with spirit,
for intellectual excellence
avoids entanglements with sentiment;
and men with educated minds
threaten the extinction of the race
for lack of educated hearts.

So I must educate my finest feelings,
for sympathy and kindliness
in hearts of multitudes through untold centuries
have moved the world
to civil law and human rights.
 Emotion
is the force sustaining justice.
 Governments will be humane and just
as long as people harbor sympathetic feelings.

The genius
of Rachmaninoff, Tschaikovsky, and Sibelius
felt the pathos of existence --
felt tragedy and triumph and wove them into music --
into symphony and song.
 But first was feeling --
flooding through the inward being --
profound and deep and moving.

Music will be music,
created or when recreated,
only as long as men are
moved
to joy and tears.

Feelings rule the universe --
brooding through the whole creation,
sweeping from the nearest atom to the farthest star,
thrilling equally to the birth of paramecia as to men --
kindling life to flame first here then there --
twinkling, emoting, blinking, evolving, moving --

Let me cultivate my finest feelings,
for these will move the world --
these will humanize my kind
into the full estate
of man.

I JUDGE MYSELF

Only selves can judge,
and using precedents of one's experience,
all judgments must be of oneself.

My faults are those
that loom so large and threatening
in the lives of others.
Knowing first hand
the disasters of deceit,
I quickly recognize
and attack deceit in others.

But my virtues
likewise find expression in the lives of others.
When I deny myself some cherished end
that someone else might have a wish fulfilled,
then I can recognize another's sacrifice
and feel a flooding warmth of kindredship.

I cannot praise
or blame
but what I praise
or blame
myself.

And, O, my judgment of another may be true;
it may be true;
the associations damning;
the evidence incriminating!
Only let me serve the verdict
on myself as well,
and with the one accused
feel my heart plummet like a stone
toward the center of the earth.

When I exalt the greatness
and the goodness in another,
seeing towers of strength,
hurricanes of power,
beacon lights of wisdom and of truth,
if I look more closely I will see
the likeness of myself
in the image of the one that I extol.

I am a fool
if I accept another's praise of me as true,
for the praise another heaps on me
is the measure of the other person's virtue
not my own.

I am misled
when I cringe before abuse
for the faults proclaimed as mine
are those of the proclaimer.
How else would the accuser know?

I may judge, then, if I wish
just so I know
I judge myself.

SNOW IN APRIL

The death of a young man in Vermont

It isn't fair
that it should snow in April,
and yet almost each year
it does.

We have just been through the winter
and we are well aware
of the immobility of ice
and the barrenness of death.

We feel deserving now of spring,
and it is dismaying
that one sees threatening black clouds
hurling balls of cotton
and feels cold wet flakes
splattering on one's face.
One resents the weather
dumping slithering sheets of sleet
on greening grass
and on crocus
that had hopefully opened petals
for the sun.

Though one knows
that friendliness, if given time,
and human sympathies
will melt the ice of this untimely slight,
yet snow in April
cuts a stinging wound into one's indignation.
We know
that winter is a part
of the cycle of the seasons.
We know
that death must come to all, to each.

But this is spring!

TO BRIM WITH LIFE

   A person
might be likened to a spring --
springs whose waters rise from hidden sources,
trickle into freshets,
dash away in turbulent brooks,
gather into rivers,
and join at last the vase expanse of sea.

   Then secretly,
mysteriously,
the ocean waters slip into the air,
and like genii form as thunder clouds over mountains,
and amid the flash of lightning and the lash of rain,
the hidden sources in the earth are kept replenished.

   Ever giving of its waters,
the spring
insures its own existence.

   And I,
by giving of my waters to the rushing stream of life,
contribute to an ever-flowing larger force
from which my spirit is renewed.

   But if I dam the outlet of my being,
the freshness of internal waters
will grow green and brackish;
my hidden source of life will then be sealed with silt;
and eventually the basin of my being
will have dried into a bowl of dust.

   To brim with life,
I must ever flow.

THE SEAS WITHIN

    Strength
to live in times like these
comes from the gift of seas within.

    As strings
of instruments ring true,
orchestras
resound with harmony.
    As each wave of sunlight
vibrates truly to itself
green growing things
can synthetize the bread of life.
    As wires
lend their tensile strength to cables,
a bridge
can span a rushing tide.

    As each string,
each wave, each wire stands alone,
the symphony sings,
the bridge upholds,
and leaves will synthetize.

    Chains
are no stronger than their weakest link,
and roofs will sag
beneath the rafters that are weak.

    Strength
comes from hills of courage
rising high within myself.
    Beauty flows
from crystal springs of my appreciation.
    Truth will gleam

from diamond hard integrity
of every inward thought and action.

   If the seas within
are calm, composed, and deep
then gifts that fortify the soul are endless;
and though a tumult clamors in the world at large,
yet a great and all pervading stillness in my person
lends a strength to live
with hope and trust.

PHOENIX-LIKE

Mysterious,
dusky, soft-footed, ever vigilant,
helpful death.
  Surely you are misunderstood, maligned.
  Let me not be one
who veils his thoughts in mourning
when he thinks of you.
  May I not imagine all the worst
of someone I have never met.

  Surely you are the great emancipator!
  If disease should overwhelm my flesh and bone
so that fever burns and pain excoriates,
you are the one
who gently cools my brow.
  If accident
should mutilate this body far beyond repair
you, it is, who takes responsibility
and thus relieves me of my obligation
to a state of uselessness.
  If age
enfeebles all my limbs
so that I am a burden to myself as well as others,
you make decisions
I am not brave enough to make.

  Yes, and too,
you are the great equalitarian.
  All privilege must yield at last
and be returned into the human heritage.
  All poverty must fall
like shackles from the poor.
  All tyrants
will be arrested in brutality.
  All the oppressed
find respite from the weight of their oppression.

The strong must yield,
the weak arise,
the wise be mystified,
the slow enlightened,
when the shadow of your dusky presence
falls upon their persons.

Before your stoicism
bribery has no value;
flattery echoes jeeringly in emptiness;
good works receive no notice;
and evil, even, cannot get attention.
Petitions go unheard,
and yet indifference cannot put you out of sight.

I seem to see
that from emancipation
new generations rise for century on century.
From equalitarianism,
opportunity is born.
Out of this namelessness,
persons rise unique in stature and in vision.
Stange as it seems,
I have arisen,
phoenix-like, from the ashes of the past.
Death has made me all I am
and offers all I hope to be.

So death,
I accept your invitation for a rendezvous,
and I will give my R.S.V.P.
to the vicissitudes of fate
to date and mail at their convenience.

With this detail attended to
I am more free to live,
knowing that when fate shall date and mail my note,
I shall meet a friend of life.

WHEN DESERT WASTES BEGIN TO BLOOM

    What is good
I would encourage
and what is evil,
I would avoid.
    But good and evil are not objects
that I meet upon the way --
good, like apples hanging from a tree --
or evil, like a stone that trips me up.
    But rather good and evil
struggle for expression from within myself,
and one or the other
temporarily commands my person.

    Evil cannot be captured,
for it is non-existence.
    Evil is the lack of tenderness --
the lack of beauty and of understanding.
    It is nothing;
and pursuit of evil with intent to capture
is of no avail.
    It is a vacuum;
and when my hands may close upon the culprit,
they clutch an emptiness.
    Futile, then, it is
for me to lie in wait to try to catch it by surprise.

    Let me turn my back
on what I think is bad,
and be concerned with what is good.
    Sympathy
must flow from out the hidden places of my being.
    Beauty
must clothe the world in which I walk.
    Helpfulness
must aid the faltering pilgrim on life's way.

Good and evil do not apply to others,
but to me.
For if I see an evil person,
evil glares from out my eyes --
eyes coldy bare of understanding.
But if I witness something good,
then in my pupils good will shine.

No.
It is not for me to separate
the wheat from tares;
it is not for me
majestically to mount the throne of moral judgment;
for though I may pronounce on others,
it is myself I place on trial.

Evil is an emptiness
that must be filled with my achievements,
truest thoughts, and gentle feelings.
Evil cannot be destroyed;
it is a barrenness to be seeded.
When desert wastes begin to bloom,
then I will see the growth of good.

SILENT CENTURIES SPEAK

I am, at times, confused.

My body is a miracle in itself --
an association of mysterious processes,
a co-operative adventure of my parts and organs.
    I am a consensus
of my million, million cells.

But consciously,
I cannot follow impulses
flashing almost instantaneously along my nerve ways,
or hail a corpuscle bearing oxygen
to the table of a hungry cell,
or set the thermostat for my central heating plant.

    And further still
I am a part of a larger body --
that of mankind.
    Man is as deep
as the centuries that stand as milestones
marking his emergence from the past.
    Man is as broad
as the host of races living on the earth
and raising hopeful faces to the sun.

    Who has created this humanity
of which I am an image?
    Voices
answering from the past are legion --
voices all around me --
voices faintly hallowing from misty distances --
voices thundering close at hand --
voices blending in a pandemonium
all together uttering "I".

    And who has made the larger livingness
from which man now takes his life?
    Multitudes
clamor in reply --
inarticulate voices answer deep from beds of coal,
from driftwood spewed upon the shore,
from geological domains of palm and pine,
from the sea, the air, the earth --
strange peepings, cadenced song, hoarse bellows,
and incoherent rumblings mingle in a single roar.

    Silent centuries speak
thunderously in the now.
    Past forms dance joyously
in configurations of the here.

TO PASS THE TEST

I came into the world
a bundle of potential.
I was an overwhelming eagerness
bent on savouring life itself.

Everything was tasted --
some to pass the test and swallowed,
and some things quickly spluttered out.

Thus bodily I became
the food that I accepted.

So too my personality has grown.
I am my land and language;
I am family, friends, and enemies;
I am my joys and sorrows,
my frustrations and accomplishments;
I am my education, nation, party;
I am my climate, rain or sunshine;
I am my mountain peaks, my rivers, plains, and oceans;
I am my customs and traditions.
I am the people --
all the people whom I have met upon my way --
the farmers, blacksmiths, teachers;
the soldiers, sailors, and marines;
the musicians, poets, actors;
the thieves, the scoundrels, drunkards;
the officials, plumbers, carpenters;
the lawyers, judges, salesmen;
the dentists, statesmen, doctors.
Yes, I am an endless pilgrimage of all these people.

But even as I grow
so too I waste away.
As times have changed,
I am the less;

As faces leave familiar circles,
I am the less;
as cars replace the horse, and planes the car,
I am the less;
as forests fall and farming lands recede,
I am the less;
as tastes and customs change,
I am the less;
as persons fail, as songs lose interest, memories fade,
I am the less;
as plants and animals are decimated
or lose primeval instinct through domestication,
I am the less;
as men hate, and war, and kill,
I am the less.

All that causes me to grow or die
has in turn been caused to grow or die
in an eternal chain.

When, then, was I born?
It almost seems as though I always was.

When will I die?
It seems that I will still be dying
long, long after I am dead.

My dated birth and death
seem unimportant,
for I am related to what has gone before,
and I will be related to what is yet to come.

Strange as it may seem,
I was dying before my birth,
and I will come to birth after I am dead.

So every birth
is my birth;
and every death
is my death.

A MOOD OF MERRIMENT

Life is a mood of merriment,
and things will come alive
as they clap their hands,
dance for joy,
and sing.

Staid straight lines of seriousness
twist and bend and weave
in configurations of the dance.
Each individual,
capriciously unique,
shatters the monotony of mental categories.

Life will not tolerate finality,
but constantly renews the earth with every morning,
every season, every species, every living thing.

Life will not plan its future,
to be indelibly designed
as patterns for the coming generations;
but whimsically life changes its direction,
confusing prophets,
and dallies with some frivolous infatuation,
invalidating schedules.

We come most alive
when stars are twinkling in the sky,
when air borne swallows soar and swoop,
when waves shimmer laughingly in sunlight on the lakes
and breakers roll and thunder on the ocean beach,
when children's laughter
pleasantly resounds upon our ears,
when colors melt and flow into each other,
when people play as well as work.

Life is a mood of merriment, like a brook --
bubbling over pebbles,
frothing in a rapids,
eddying in swirling pools,
and then gliding silently between its banks.

But to sit in gloom,
to dim the twinkle in one's eye
with a stare of grave concern,
to drop the corners of one's mouth below one's chin,
to be unduly serious
is to die before one's time.

Give freedon to your spirit, then,
that it may soar
and dance
and sing.

A WORK OF ART

A person's body
is an instrument of strings
that vibrates to the music of emotions.
As one tunes one's body
to the joys and pathos of humanity,
it transmits exciting melodies --
joyful, sad, nostalgic,
melodies passed on to others
and to future generations.

A person's mind
is a canvas on which one paints
the mountain peaks of one's ideals,
landscapes of knowledge,
stars of understanding
that twinkle in the sky of human thought,
as life rolls on beneath it.

A person's heart
is a poem.
The rhythmic beat of sympathy
is the meter of its lines.
The rhyming verse of love
is in its endings.
The ecstasy of experience
is in the beauty it portrays.

Yes,
humanity is a work of art.
　It is an instrument of music
played by the sweeping fingers of emotion.
　It is a painter's canvas
exhibiting the noblest yearnings of the race.
　It is a poem
rhymed and metered
in empathy and love.

　A multitude of lives
have sung their songs and gone to rest.
　A host of persons
have inscribed their visions on the scroll of time,
before their fingers failed
and dropped the pen.
　Teeming myriads have lived and loved
this same humanity in which I now rejoice,
before their waves subsided into stillness.

　To be a person
I, too, must labor at my art.

LAUGH OR CRY

In contemplating man,
this thing I am,
I do not know if I should laugh or cry.

Though man declares
he is the apple of the eye of God,
yet in the image of himself he made his deity;
so he is mirrored as the apple of his self appreciation.

Though man declares
the universe is patterned as his mind is patterned,
yet he would laugh to scorn
a monkey, who, if it could speak,
might claim the universe
was measured out exactly to the length and thickness
of a monkey's tail.

Though man declares
that he alone has been bequeathed dominion of the earth,
yet he cannot regulate himself,
much less the living things that he commands.

But I am man,
and I have within myself an irrepressible conceit,
and the record of an inveterate impostor.

Through all the history of man,
the earth has trembled
with the measured tread of marching fighting men.
    Through all of history
resounds one horrendous disharmony and din --
the clash of smashing swords,
and splintering scream of spears,
the crackling of musketry,
the belching bellow of the cannon,
the whoosh of weapons throwing flame.

the jarring blast of block-busting bombs,
the typewriting chatter of automatic guns,
and now the instant, searing screech and wham
of atom bombs.
  All the waste and ruin,
all the human tragedy and tears,
the wail of relatives and friends,
the bitterness, the aching of this senselessness.

  But I am man,
and this destructiveness
leaps for release within me
like a maddened dog upon a leash.

  Yet, men have made amends.

  Men of peace have given up their lives
for the sake of freedom and good-will;
men have brought to birth
a new breath-taking beauty
in the work of artists, poets, and musicians;
they have ennobled human feelings
in service to their fellow men --
through medicine, assistance, charities;
men have deepened knowledge, broadened wisdom,
sharpened wit;
men have devised the golden rule,
enforced observance through the rule of law,
and specified its aims
in bills of rights and catalogues of human rights;
men have mourned, despaired, repented, loved,
forgiven, trusted;
they have erected democratic governments,
launched the United Nations, and sought for peace.

  I am man
and this is I as well.

Perhaps the latitude of life is a pendulum
that for man swings farther to each side.

But hopefully,
the longitude of life is a process of rebirth,
a starting from beginnings for every living thing,
and in each individual
moving just a bit beyond man's former limits.
Hopefully,
life is a process of rebirth,
and love
is now the new horizon
for the present generations of mankind.

Yes, hopefully,
life is a process of rebirth for each and all,
and peace is now the challenge of our times.

JOYOUSLY POSSESSED

In the elemental processes
an overwhelming ardor
brings existent things to be.
And these creations will exist
as long as they are joyously possessed,
but when they lie unused,
they atrophy and rust away.

Wings were born
when creatures yearned
to free their beings from the clutch of earth
and to rise into the wind.
And wings will fill the air
as long as birds will mount the windy summits of the sky,
veer joyfully into the blustering of storms,
and sail into the gold of sunset.
But if their ardor fails,
then wings are lost,
for things unused eventually are useless,
and finally one's last resort
may be to hide one's head beneath the sand.

Man's cup of life
will be no fuller than he fills it,
and he must fill it for himself.

To be
one must be possessed
by ardor.

WINGS OF THE SPIRIT

Though I am bound to earth in body,
yet in spirit
I laugh along the sky with capering clouds.

Though I walk the surface of the earth in body,
yet in spirit
I stride over mountain peaks,
and step from star to star.

Though in body
I express myself imperfectly to my fellow men,
in spirit I whisper secrets to my larger self.

In body I am bound by the past,
but in spirit I burst into the future,
dreaming splendid dreams of what is to be.

In body I must sit upon a hill,
but in spirit my longings mingle with sunset colors
and fade into the treasury of night.

In body I am but one in a multitude,
in spirit I am a multitude in one.

Let me pause in my haste,
and learn again
to dream the long, long dreams of youth.

Let me capture in my heart the song of a bird
that sings again in drowsy reveries.

Let me thrill to the fragrance of apple blossoms
and bathe the spirit in the blue of the sky.

Let me venture forth on wings of the spirit
searching for new delights
to bring home to earth.

SO SWING

All of existence flows;
life is change.
But when I crystalize into rigidity,
then I fall like sediment
to lie inert upon the bottom of the flow of things.

If one could cage the winds,
they would be still.
If water does not flow,
it soon grows green.
If change no longer kneads my body,
it will be dead.

So swing,
swing in your orbits,
swing earth and galaxies,
swing electrons, moon, and stars;
change your relationships, move, revolve!

Contract, O earth;
heave mountains high into the sky,
dredge valleys in the seams,
explode volcanoes,
slosh the seas about the land,
grade the surface flat with ice,
tip back and forth to alternate the seasons!

Blow, then, O wind, blow;
erode the mountains, sway the trees,
bring summer, winter, spring and fall.
Blow season after season.

Rain --
rain in torrents --
flood the rivers, fill the seas.

Change, living things;
grow, mutate, evolve --
multiply the species,
build more complicated individuals,
increase the faculties of sensation,
improve the quality of organs.
  Grow and multiply!

Fly by, O years, fly by;
though changes come,
though hair grows grey and strength may fade,
yet this is life,
and when the changes stop, whether soon or late,
I will be no more.

Bend, pride of mine,
bend your stiffened neck,
acknowledge error, laugh at yourself,
let down your guard.
  Too much needs the doing
to waste my energy to try
to stem the tide of things.
  Besides that stiffened neck
burns bright red in summer
and whitens with the cold in winter.
  Pull it in!

And fear, go on away;
let me plunge in, let go, enjoy the swim,
trust the buoyancy of water, trust myself,
trust the guarding help of others.
  Shake hands!
Strangers are only unknown friends.
  Smile at enemies;
they are but myself,
reacting as I do.

    An enemy is only I
contesting what is worst within myself.
    Fear only hamstrings my expression;
so trust, plunge in, shake hands, and smile!

www.ingramcontent.com/pod-product-compliance
Lightning Source LLC
Chambersburg PA
CBHW071622170426
43195CB00038B/1993